Style & Substance

A quick reference guide to punctuation using the wisdom of the ages for examples

Craig Hattersley
Cow House Media
Austin, Texas 78735

Style & Substance: A quick reference guide to punctuation using the wisdom of the ages for examples

ISBN: 978-0-9915296-0-5 (eBook)
0991529618 (print)

Cow House Media
5605 Oak Boulevard, Austin, Texas 78735

All rights reserved. No part of this book may be reproduced or transmitted in any form or by any means, electronic, mechanical, photocopying, recording, or otherwise, without the express written permission of the publisher. For information, contact the author.

Contents

Introduction v
Apostrophe 1
Colon 5
Commas 9
Dash 25
Ellipses 31
Exclamation Points 35
Hyphens 39
Parentheses 49
Periods 53
Question Marks 55
Semicolons 57

Introduction

This manual sprung from an effort in the mid-'80s to standardize punctuation for *3rd Coast,* an upstart, avant city magazine for Austin, Texas—a publication that twice made the finals of the National Magazine Awards. I read proofs, then copy, eventually landing as senior editor on the strength of an anal tendency towards composition. This had evolved in my final semesters finishing a degree at the University of Texas.

I had returned to school to finish a BS in journalism, the path of least resistance given the hours I had accumulated at Syracuse University in years past and various sojourns in the field. I fancied myself already the accomplished writer and so determined to take every possible writing course—in the English as well as Journalism departments—to merely polish my chops while piling up the requisite credits.

I coasted through much of this return to academia, relying on my relative maturity and all the flash and dazzle of a literary dandy, then swaggered into the upper reaches of composition in the English department—the domain of the plenipotentate of prose, John Trimble. Therein I discovered, in two humbling ventures into advanced expository writing—his 325M and 379C—the untutored gonzo that lived within.

In his quiet scholarly manner, John taught me the beauty of the well-fashioned phrase, the obsessive quest for *le mot juste* (in quiet contrast to the bluster that had so thoroughly plastered my prose). In short, he taught me what it meant to write with style: It's not only *what* you say, but how you say it.

And fundamental to style, a careful writer must exercise a clear and consistent use of punctuation to lead the reader unerringly word to word, sentence to sentence, along the path to clarity. Yet the question then remains, What constitutes good style in punctuation? Different stylebooks vary wildly in its definition, depending on what kind of audience you address. The weighty tome of a scholarly journal assumes a far different demeanor than found in the gabble of tabloid journalism. What's a student of style to do? What follows is an attempt to sift through the various rules covering punctuation to compile an easy-to-read manual for the careful writer.

One last prefatory word. The trend nowadays is toward minimizing punctuation, especially commas, in the interest of swift, uncluttered prose. Whenever "open punctuation" makes the reader's task easier, we endorse it wholeheartedly. But as a number of stylebooks note, punctuation can be used to make a sentence clearer or easier to read, or can contribute to the overall tone and pace of the prose, and shouldn't be sacrificed just for the sake of minimizing keystrokes.

Apostrophe

Generally, the apostrophe is used to form contractions, plurals, and possessives, as well as to indicate omissions. On possessives, newspapers (and some magazines) don't add an -s after the apostrophe when the word ends in -s (Texas', Lois', Jones'). In certain exceptions to this style, usually foreign names, the -s is silent and thus will take an -s after the apostrophe (Francois's, Rabelais's, Des Moines's, Arkansas's). Other magazines and most book publishers add the -s in all cases.

- If you want to show common possession by two coordinate nouns (e.g., John and Mary), one apostrophe will do the trick (John and Mary's house). But for separate possession, separate apostrophes should be used (John's and Mary's clothes).

- In forming the plurals of uppercase letters, acronyms, numbers, words standing for numbers, or the like, an apostrophe isn't needed:

    the ABCs, two PhDs, the three Rs, three As and two Bs, a column of twos, back in the 1920s, the roaring '20s, three B52s, shot in the low 80s, count off by fours, no ifs or ands about it, if there were no CIAs or KGBs . . .

    Note that we favor using uppercase for letters standing alone (e.g., "mind your Ps and Qs"), adding the apostrophe only where there might otherwise be confusion. Other stylebooks prefer using the lowercase and apostrophe (e.g., "mind your p's and q's").

- Use an apostrophe with indefinite pronouns (e.g., "someone") but not with possessive pronouns:

    someone's car, each other's numbers, a friend of hers, a friend of theirs

"Be steadfast as a tower that doth not bend its stately summit to the tempest's shock."
—Dante Alighieri

- While the possessive of most common nouns is formed by adding -'s, some expressions ending in -s (or an "s" sound) form the possessive by adding the apostrophe alone:

    for old times' sake, for goodness' sake, for conscience' sake, for appearance' sake, for convenience' sake

- Don't use an apostrophe with shortened formations such as *though, till, round, chute, possum,* or *phone.* They've all become upstanding members of the English language and can stand on their own.

- In some informal prose, capital letters are combined as a verb form, necessitating the use of an apostrophe, though this form is mostly used in newspaper headlines:

    The champ KO'd the kid.

Apostrophe

>   Vanna White was MC'ing the show (but "emceeing" is preferred).

>   The House OK's that kind of behavior (but "okays" is preferred).

- Be wary of the genitive case: It's similar to the possessive and formed the same way. In general, these phrases involve measures of time and space. Several idiomatic expressions take this form:

  > a day's wages, two hours' travel, an hour's delay, a hair's breadth, a stone's throw, in three days' time

- One obscure construction involving the possessive should be noted. It goes by the ponderous name "genitive with gerund." A gerund is the participle of a verb (*singing, walking*) used as a noun. In the sentence "Walking in the rain seems beyond the call of duty," you wouldn't add "they" at the front ("They walking in the rain . . ."). This construction takes the old genitive: "Their walking in the rain. . . ." Similarly:

  > Their [not they] leaving the meeting is inexcusable.

  > I'm upset over my friend's [not friend] wrecking his car.

  > He had never given a thought to its [not it] not being legal.

  In some cases, however, the construction resists use of the possessive:

  > Human history is the sad result of each one looking out for himself.
  > —Julio Cortazar

Colon

In general, the colon implies *that is, namely, this is what that means,* or even *for example*. If you don't mean the sentence to stop dead, don't use a colon. Stylebooks caution that it is not inserted between a verb and its object or a preposition and its object:

> The office of the scholar is [no colon] to cheer, to raise, and to guide men by showing them facts amidst appearances.
> —Ralph Waldo Emerson

> Every man of action has a strong dose of [no colon] egotism, pride, hardness, and cunning.
> —Charles DeGaulle

> Simple narcissism gives the power of beasts to [no colon] politicians, professional wrestlers, and female movie stars.
> —Norman Mailer

- The first word after a colon should be capped when it begins a complete sentence. Not all stylebooks agree on this, but we feel that this type of signposting aids the reader in readily discerning the sentence flow from the structure.

> There're two people in the world that are not likeable: a master and a slave.
> — Nikki Giovanni

- The terms *as follows* and *the following* require a colon if followed by enumerated items:

> The steps are as follows:
> 1. Bend over at your desk
> 2. Put your head between your legs. . . .

Sometimes, however, these terms don't lead right into the list. When another sentence intervenes, a period before the list suffices:

> An outline of the method follows. Note that care was taken to remove any elements of truth.
> 1. Identical amounts of hearsay were gathered
> 2. All witnesses were taken out of the sample. . . .

✸ In general, a colon is used to introduce quotations when the quoted matter is more than one sentence long. If the quote is one sentence, a comma is used:

> Mencken said, "The great artists of the world are never Puritans, and seldom even ordinarily respectable."
>
> —H. L. Mencken

> Albert Schweitzer once wrote: "Affirmation of life is the spiritual act by which man ceases to live unreflectively and begins to devote himself to his life with reverence in order to raise it to its true value. To affirm life is to deepen, to make more inward, and to exalt the will to live."
>
> —Albert Schweitzer

Colon

The colon, however, may also be used to introduce a supporting or contributing quote following a complete clause:

> The squalor of the streets reminded him of a line from Oscar Wilde: "We are all in the gutter, but some of us are looking at the stars."
> —Oscar Wilde

> The man who listens to Reason is lost: Reason enslaves all whose minds are not strong enough to master her.
> —George Bernard Shaw

> Puritanism: The haunting fear that someone, somewhere, may be happy.
> — H. L. Mencken

- Colons also act as dividers in certain circumstances, such as in time (10:30, 3:45); elapsed time, as in a race (1:32:45:6, 1:32:46); or in Biblical references (Matthew 2:6, Luke 4:3).

"No man ever believes that the Bible means what it says: He is always convinced that it says what he means."
—George Bernard Shaw

Commas

Commas bedevil even experienced writers. Small wonder, since no two stylebooks agree exactly where they should go. Often, commas are optional, inserted at will by the author in the interest of clarity or pacing. Commas represent the briefest of pauses in sentence flow—the smallest interruption in continuity of thought or sentence structure. Some stylebooks say that a comma should be used only if it makes the meaning clearer or aids in sentence flow. But this approach may cause as many problems as it solves.

John Trimble, in *Writing With Style* (3e), advocates a more commonsense approach: "Insert a comma wherever there is a light natural pause. Test it this way: Read your sentence aloud, in a measured voice, as if to a large audience. If you find that you naturally pause in a given place, or must pause to make the sense of your sentence instantly intelligible to the listener, insert a comma. Let your ear and good sense be your guides."

- The abbreviations *i.e., etc.,* and *e.g.* are parenthetical and should be set off by commas:

    Just as we outgrow a pair of trousers, we outgrow acquaintances, libraries, principles, etc., at times before they're worn out.
    —Georg Lichtenberg

- The abbreviations *Jr., Sr.,* and *III* ("the third") are restrictive, according to modern usage, and shouldn't be set off by commas. Similarly, omit the commas before add-ons such as *Inc.* and *Ltd.* These commas add pointless clutter.

    Harry Hurt III, Sammy Davis Jr., Time-Life Inc., Real Life Ltd.

    If, however, you choose to use the comma before, you must also add one aft.

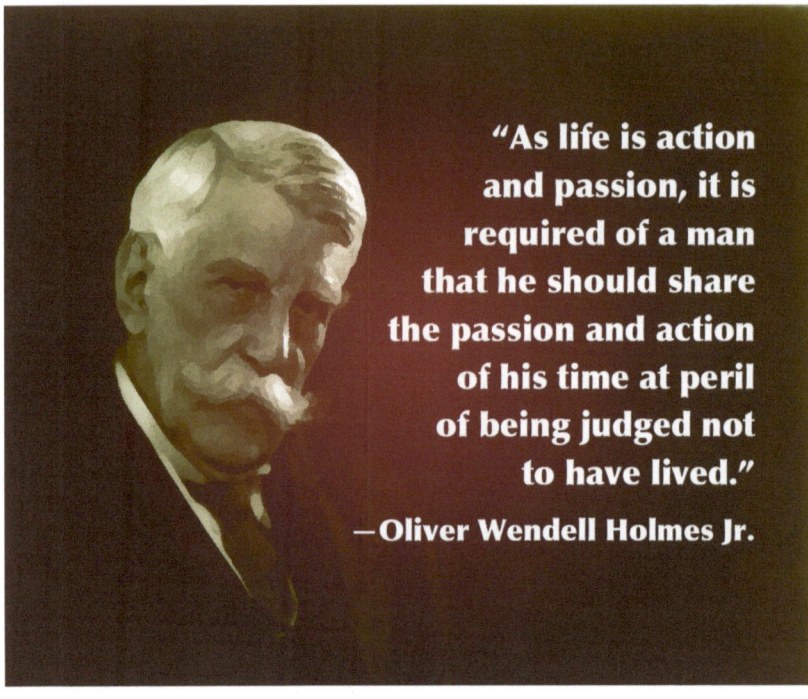

"As life is action and passion, it is required of a man that he should share the passion and action of his time at peril of being judged not to have lived."
—Oliver Wendell Holmes Jr.

- The words *which*, *where*, and *when* often begin nonrestrictive clauses. Where so, they require a comma:

  When poverty comes in at the door, love flies out the window.
  —17th-century saying

  When power leads man toward arrogance, poetry reminds him of his limitations.
  —John F. Kennedy

  Where necessity ends, curiosity begins.
  —Samuel Johnson

  When it is dark enough, you can see the stars.
  — Ralph Waldo Emerson

  Laws should be like death, which spares no one.
  —Montesquieu

- The comma splice—fusing two independent clauses with a comma instead of a comma-plus-conjunction—is an illiteracy. It's permis-

Commas

sible only when the clauses are short and close in form:

No: Art, like life, should be free, both are experimental.
Yes: Art, like life, should be free; both are experimental.

Or: Art, like life, should be free, since both are experimental.
—George Santayana

But:

Man proposes, God disposes.
—Thomas A Kempis

Act quickly, think slowly.
—Greek proverb

The scholar seeks, the artist finds.
—Andre Gide

Let us prefer, let us not exclude.
—Joseph Raux

A young man is a theory, an old man is a fact.
—Edgar Watson Howe

- A phrase of attribution should be set off from the rest of the sentence by commas:

    According to Robert Frost, education is hanging around until you've caught on.

    "Fanaticism," Santayana wrote, "consists in redoubling your efforts when you have forgotten your aim."
    —George Santayana

    Note that commas (as well as periods) always go before the closing quotation mark(s), whether single, double, or both.

- Words in apposition should be set off by commas. By "apposition," we mean a noun or noun phrase placed with another as an explanatory equivalent:

    Promise, large promise, is the soul of an advertisement.
    —Samuel Johnson

    Rough work, iconoclasm, but the only way to get at truth.
    —Oliver Wendell Holmes Sr.

> The truth, the hope of any time, must always be sought in minorities.
> —Ralph Waldo Emerson

Similarly, figures in apposition, as in a baseball score, should be set off by commas. Many stylebooks say that if the score appears at the end of a sentence, the comma is optional.

> The house passed the bill, 202 to 22, after a free-swinging debate on the floor.

> In extra innings, the Yankees beat the Red Sox, 4-3.

> Or: In extra innings, the Yankees beat the Red Sox 4-3.

❖ In elliptical constructions, a comma may often substitute for a missing word or words. Note in the first example that the comma substitutes for the words *is the test:*

> Fire is the test of gold; adversity, of strong men.
> —Seneca

> An honest man speaks the truth, though it may give offence; a vain man, in order that it may.
> — William Hazlitt

> Men have sight; women, foresight.
> —Victor Hugo

When the construction is clear enough without punctuation, omit the comma:

> Solitude is impracticable, and society fatal.
> —Ralph Waldo Emerson

> Art helps nature, and experience art.
> —Thomas Fuller

> Society is produced by our wants and government by our wickedness.
> —Thomas Paine

> Justice consists of doing no one injury, decency in giving no one offense.
> — Marcus T. Cicero

> Our frailties are invincible, our virtues barren; the battle goes sore against us to the going down of the sun.
> —Robert Louis Stevenson

Commas

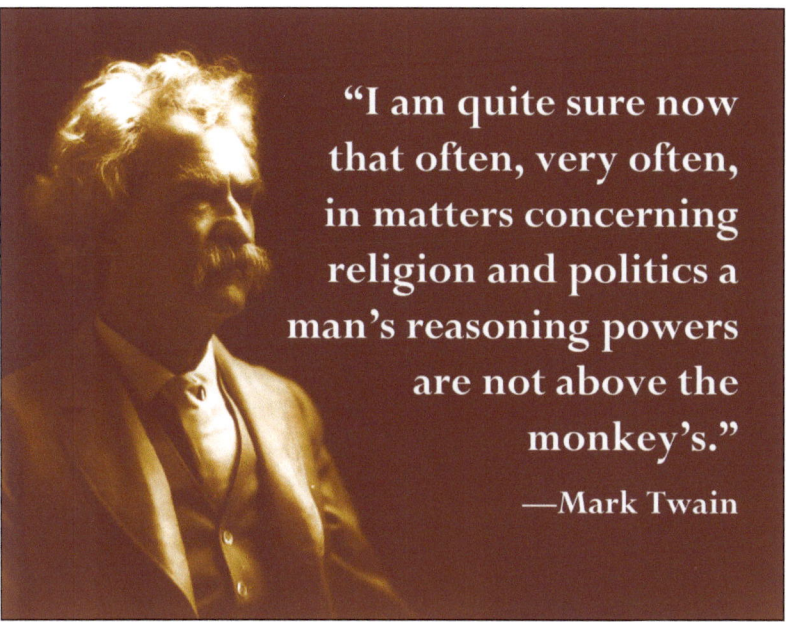

"I am quite sure now that often, very often, in matters concerning religion and politics a man's reasoning powers are not above the monkey's."
—Mark Twain

This construction is sometimes incorrectly hybridized as follows:

The cooking is traditional and the portions large.

Note that the verb for the second clause should be *are*, not *is*.

- Omit commas in measures of height, weight, time, and latitude. Note that in measurements (depth, height, length, and width), newspaper (and some magazine) style calls for numerals instead of words.

    4 feet 9 inches

    13 pounds 5 ounces

    10 hours 30 minutes latitude 19 degrees north

    latitude 32 degrees 14 minutes north

- In the following examples, a good argument can be made that the proper names should be set off by commas. Yes, they are in apposition to the nouns preceding them, but is there a real danger of misunderstanding? In normal conversation, few people

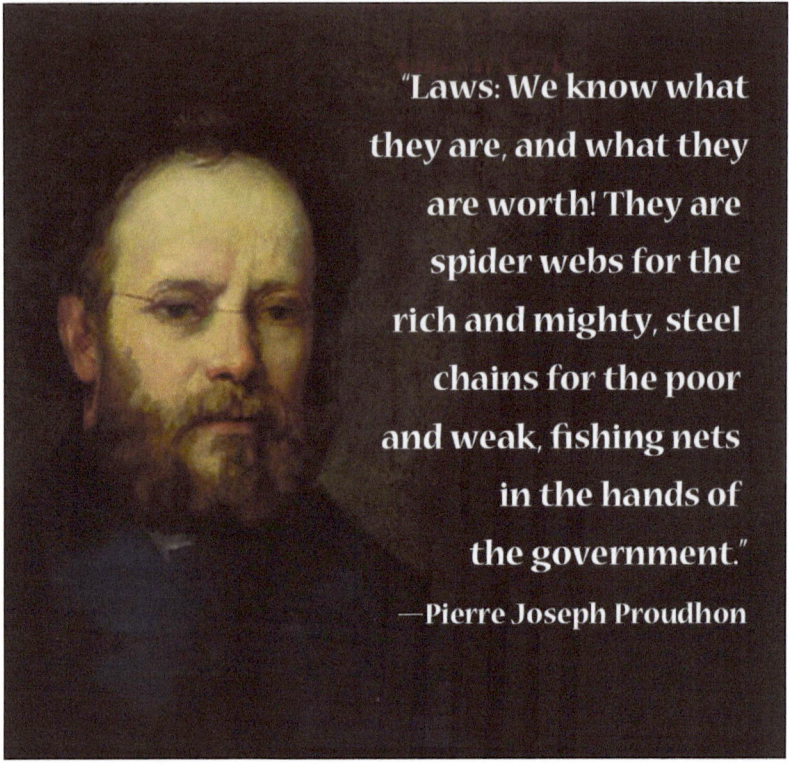

"Laws: We know what they are, and what they are worth! They are spider webs for the rich and mighty, steel chains for the poor and weak, fishing nets in the hands of the government."
—Pierre Joseph Proudhon

pause before and after the name; hence, most publications favoring open punctuation omit the commas:

My brother Tom and I went to the council meeting.

My wife Jan met them at the airport.

- Often, commas may be omitted with short transitional or introductory expressions. One suggested rule of thumb says that if an introductory expression runs more than five words, a comma is inserted to ensure instant comprehension:

Without grace beauty is an unbaited hook.
—French proverb

Under democracy one party always devotes its chief energies to trying to prove that the other party is unfit to rule—and both commonly succeed, and are right.
—H. L. Mencken

Commas

> Human history becomes more and more a race between education and catastrophe.
> —H. G. Wells

> I have discovered that we may be in some degree whatever character we choose.
> —James Boswell

> Where true religion has prevented one crime, false religions have afforded a pretext for a thousand.
> —Charles Colton

> If you ask me what I came to do in this world, I, an artist, I will answer you, "I am here to live outloud."
> —Emile Zola

- Commas generally set off interjections, transitional adverbs, and similar elements that create a distinct break in continuity:

> There is only one religion, though there are a hundred versions of it.
> —George Bernard Shaw

> Personality, too, is destiny.
> —Erik Erikson

> Adapt or perish, now as ever, is Nature's inexorable imperative.
> —H. G. Wells

> Starvation, and not sin, is the parent of modern crime.
> —Oscar Wilde

> Il seems that in advanced stages of stupidity, a lack of ideas is compensated for by an excess of ideologies.
> —Carlos Ruiz Zafon

While *though* should always be set off by commas when used internally, *indeed* and *in fact* may be used with or without commas, depending on the emphasis desired:

> If ignorance is indeed bliss, it is a very low grade of the article.
> —Tehyl Hsieh

> I am, indeed, a king, because I know how to rule myself.
> —Pietro Aretino

- Long adverbial phrases usually take a comma when they precede the subject. The comma is dropped, however, when they follow the predicate:

   > Without wearing any mask we are conscious of, we have a special face for each friend.
   > —Oliver Wendell Holmes Sr.

   > For an impenetrable shield, stand inside yourself.
   > —Henry David Thoreau

   > The religions are obsolete when the reforms do not proceed from them.
   > —Ralph Waldo Emerson

   > I tremble for my country when I reflect that God is just.
   > —Thomas Jefferson

As in other introductory phrases, commas may be omitted in short adverbial phrases:

> After three days men grow weary of a wench, a guest, and rainy weather.
> —Ben Franklin

> In the race for money some men may come first, but man comes last.
> —Marya Mannes

> By too much sitting still the body becomes unhealthy; and soon the mind.
> —Henry Wadsworth Longfellow

A comma should not be used after an introductory adverbial phrase that immediately precedes the verb it modifies:

> With the catching end the pleasures of the chase.
> —Abraham Lincoln

> In the history of the individual is always an account of his condition, and he knows himself to be a party to his present estate.
> —Ralph Waldo Emerson

> Only in men's imagination does every truth find an effective and undeniable existence.
> —Joseph Conrad

Commas

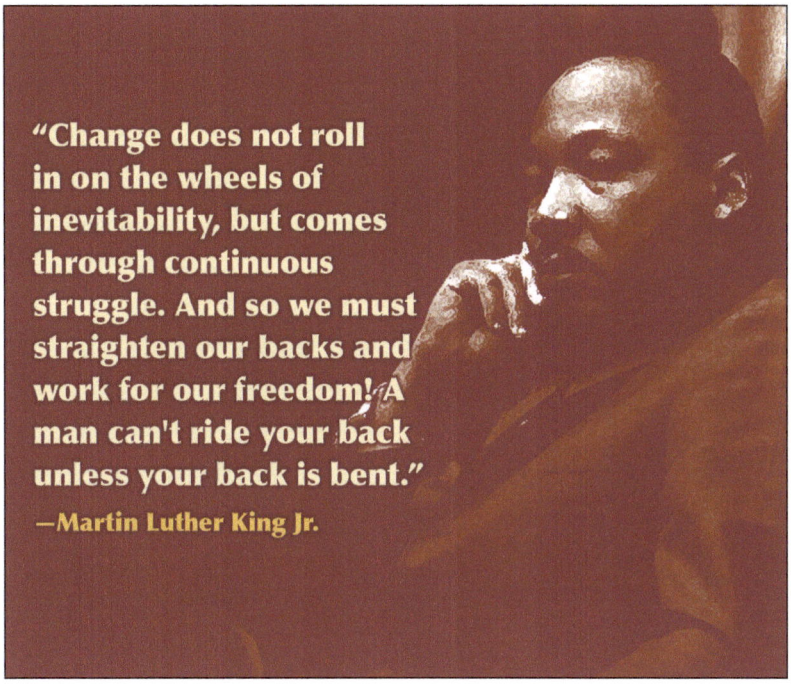

"Change does not roll in on the wheels of inevitability, but comes through continuous struggle. And so we must straighten our backs and work for our freedom! A man can't ride your back unless your back is bent."
—Martin Luther King Jr.

An adverbial phrase that interrupts a subject and its predicate is usually set off by commas:

> The law, in its majesty equality, forbids the rich as well as the poor to sleep under bridges, to beg in the streets, and to steal bread.
> —Anatole France

○ An introductory participial phrase should be set off unless it immediately precedes, and forms part of, the verb:

> Obsessed by a fairy tale, we spend our lives searching for a magic door and a lost kingdom of peace.
> —Eugene O'Neill

> An honest heart being the first blessing, a knowing head is the second.
> —Thomas Jefferson

> Believing in Hell must distort every judgment on this life.
> —Cyril Connolly

Taking sides is the beginning of sincerity, and earnestness follows shortly afterwards, and the human being becomes a bore.
—Oscar Wilde

One caveat: An all-too-common mistake with participial phrases leaves them dangling without a proper subject to modify. Trimble provides a good example:

Coming out of Safeway, a dog bit him on the leg.

Unless the dog came from within the store to assault the gentleman, the sentence is miscast. The introductory phrase modifies the subject of the sentence.

Commas

- If two phrases within a sentence modify the same word—that is, have a common termination point—commas should be used to distinguish them:

    > Glory ought to be the consequence, not the motive, of our actions.
    > —Pliny the Younger

    > In giving advice seek to help, not to please, your friend.
    > —Solon

- Commas are used to set off words in direct address:

    > A man, sir, should keep his friendship in constant repair.
    > —Samuel Johnson

    > Hell, madame, is to love no longer.
    > —Georges Bernanos

    > Sir, a man may be so much of everything, that he is nothing of anything.
    > — Samuel Johnson

    > Be good, sweet maid, and let who will be clever.
    > —Charles Kingsley

- Commas should set off alternate meanings of words, commonly in the form of appositive-plus-conjunction:

    > All sins have their origin in a sense of inferiority, otherwise called ambition.
    > —Cesare Pavese

    > We who live in prison, and in whose lives there is no event but sorrow, have to measure time by throbs of pain, and the record of bitter moments.
    > —Oscar Wilde

    > The great man, that is, the man most imbued with the spirit of the time, is the impressionable man.
    > —Ralph Waldo Emerson

- An antithetical phrase or clause, often beginning with *not*, should be set off if it isn't essential to the meaning of the modified element:

    > In moderating, not in satisfying, desires, lies peace.
    > —Reginald Heber

God looks at the clean hands, not the full ones.
—Publilius Syrus

Human progress is furthered, not by conformity, but by aberration.
—H. L. Mencken

It is not love that should be depicted as blind, but self-love.
—Voltaire

The spirit in which a thing is given determines that in which the debt is acknowledged; it's the intention, not the face value of the gift, that's weighed.
—Seneca

It is his nature, not his standing, that makes the good man.
—Publilius Syrus

Virtue has its own reward, but no sales at the box office.
—Mae West

- Antithetical clauses that depend on each other to make sense should be separated:

    The more things a man is ashamed of, the more respectable he is.
    —George Bernard Shaw

    The greater intellect one has, the more originality one finds in men. Ordinary persons find no difference between men.
    —Blaise Pascal

    The more we see, the more we must be able to imagine, and the more we imagine, the more we must think we see.
    —Gotthold Lessing

    Gratitude is a debt which usually goes on accumulating like blackmail; the more you pay, the more is exacted.
    —Mark Twain

Short ones, though, don't require commas:

The more the merrier.

The sooner the better.

Culture is one thing and varnish is another.
—Ralph Waldo Emerson

Commas

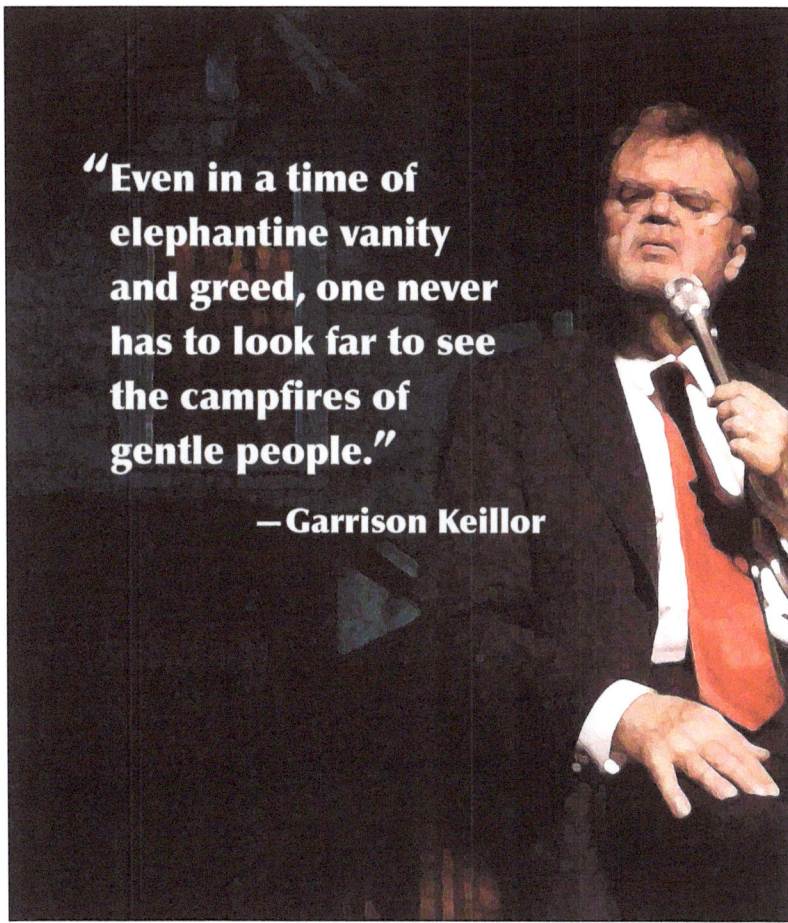

"Even in a time of elephantine vanity and greed, one never has to look far to see the campfires of gentle people."
—Garrison Keillor

○ Sometimes a comma is inserted to prevent the reader from mistakenly joining two words or clauses:

To Mike, Anthony remained a mystery.

Soon after, the truck pulled out of the garage.

To the courageous, men turn with respect.

Similarly, it's often necessary to separate two like words with a comma, even though not otherwise required by the syntax:

Let's march in, in columns of fours.

Whatever is, is okay by me.

In 1970, 200 editors attended.

- Use commas to set off the different elements of an address. Note that numbers in a street address do not take commas:

    He sent it to 12456 Farfel Drive, Billings, Montana.

    She moved from Washington, D.C., to Texas.

    New York, New York, remains the hub of activity.

- Use commas in dates, except when writing just the month and year:

    June 6, 1944, was D-Day.

    She left in June 1980.

- If a quotation is used as either the subject of the sentence or the object of the verb, no comma is used:

    If we ever pass out as a great nation we ought to put on our tombstone "America died from a delusion that she had moral leadership."
    —Will Rogers

- A comma is frequently used to set off a question from the clause that introduces it:

    In Boston they ask, How much does he know? In New York, How much is he worth? In Philadelphia, Who were his parents?
    —Mark Twain

In indirect discourse or with rhetorical, unspoken, or imaginary questions, no quotation marks are used, though other punctuation may be retained:

What am I doing here? she wondered.

History says, if it pleases, Excuse me, I beg your pardon, it will never happen again if I can help it.
—Carl Sandburg

The words *yes* and *no* and other such words should not be quoted except in direct discourse:

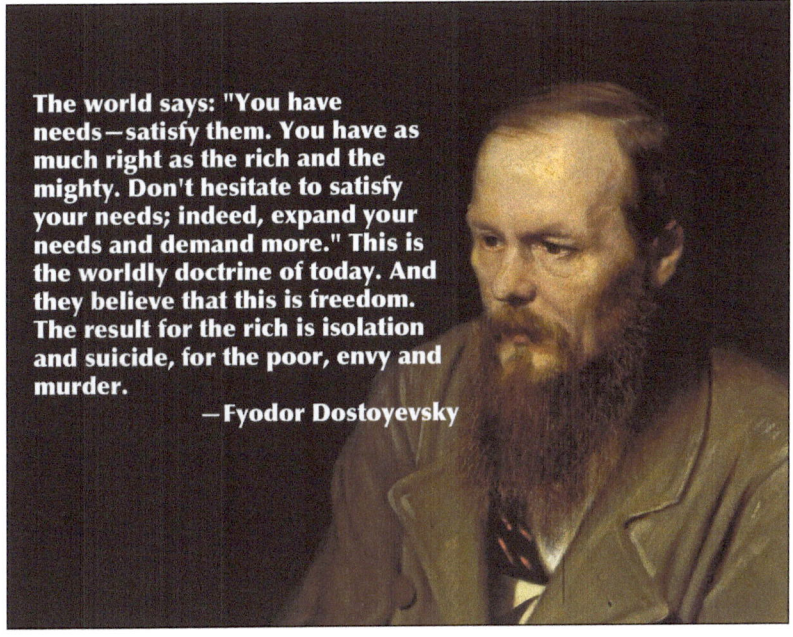

> The world says: "You have needs—satisfy them. You have as much right as the rich and the mighty. Don't hesitate to satisfy your needs; indeed, expand your needs and demand more." This is the worldly doctrine of today. And they believe that this is freedom. The result for the rich is isolation and suicide, for the poor, envy and murder.
> —Fyodor Dostoyevsky

To say yes, you have to sweat and roll up your sleeves and plunge both hands into life up to the elbows. It is easy to say no, even if saying no means death.
—Jean Anouilh

Don't ask me why.

"Why?" she asked again.

- Don't use a comma before the conjunction *that* in sentences constructed like the following (for clarity, a comma may be inserted after the phrase):

    The authorities believe that with average crime rates it will still be a problem.

    It can be easily demonstrated that when such importance is attached to each game, the pressure can mount unbearably.

- The down style calls nowadays for a "smoothing out" of certain compound sentences:

    In the morning, the majority of the students left campus, and unless I'm misinformed, there shouldn't be any further protest.

Here, the clause "unless I'm misinformed" is dependent on the second half of the compound sentence. Up-style punctuation would place a comma before "unless."

- Book publishers and many magazines use the "serial comma" in enumerative series such as "a, b, and c." (The serial comma is the one directly before the conjunction introducing the final element in a series.) While most newspapers (and some magazines), intent on saving space, insist on omitting that comma (thus making it "a, b and c"), the practice often results in confusion. We prefer a "one rule fits all" approach, in the interest of both clarity and consistency. For a particularly cogent discussion of the issue, see Wilson Follett's *Modern American Usage*.

> You never will be the person you can be if pressure, tension, and discipline are taken out of your life.
> — James G. Bilkey

> For every complex problem, there is a solution that is simple, neat, and wrong.
> —H. L. Mencken

Dash

When used singly, dashes indicate abrupt changes in thought, continuity, and pace, or sum up elements at the end of a sentence. When used in pairs (a construction known as the "double dash"), they set off a parenthetical statement. The dash is typewritten as two hyphens with no space fore and aft (word--word).

- Use a dash to indicate a sharp turn in thought, a significant pause, or uncertainty:

    I don't know where—ah, there she is now.

    After four years he came back—as an apprentice!

    I—I think so.

    "It'll never—" She suddenly stopped.

    "If only I had—" "The time?" "—the backing of the workers."

- When a quoted sentence in direct discourse is interrupted by phrases that aren't part of the quotation, dashes are used to separate the added material:

    "My little friend"—his voice showed concern—"I'm afraid he's gone."

- Pairs of dashes are used to indicate apposition, particularly where commas might be confusing, or where more emphasis is sought, or where the material within the appositive is lengthy and requires signposting to bring the reader back to the main point of the sentence:

    It's a naive, domestic burgundy—with absolutely no breeding—but I think you'll be amused by its presumption.

    —James Thurber

> Remember always that all of us—and you and I especially—are descended from immigrants and revolutionists.
> —Franklin D. Roosevelt

> The nearest way to glory—a short cut, as it were—is to strive to be what you wish to be thought to be.
> —Socrates

Similarly, dashes or pairs of dashes are used in enumeration:

> The lust for comfort—that stealthy thing that enters the house a guest, and then becomes a host, and then a master.
> —Kahlil Gibran

> This is the artist, then—life's hungry man, the glutton of eternity, beauty's miser, glory's slave.
> —Thomas Wolfe

> The shrewd guess, the fertile hypothesis, the courageous leap to a tentative conclusion—these are the most valuable coin of the thinker at words.
> —Jerome Bruner

Another form of enumeration uses a dash to set off an element for emphasis or explanation. In this case, the dash means *that is:*

> We live as we dream—alone.
> —Joseph Conrad

> The greatest obstacle to discovery is not ignorance—it is the illusion of knowledge.
> — Daniel J. Boorstin

> Naturalness is the easiest thing in the world to acquire, if you will forget yourself—forget about the impression you are trying to make.
> — Dale Carnegie

> TV—chewing gum for the eyes.
> —Frank Lloyd Wright

> The intellectual world is divided into two classes—dilettantes, on the one hand, and pedants, on the other.
> —Miguel de Unamuno

> In those days he was wiser than he is now—he used frequently to take my advice.
> —Winston Churchill

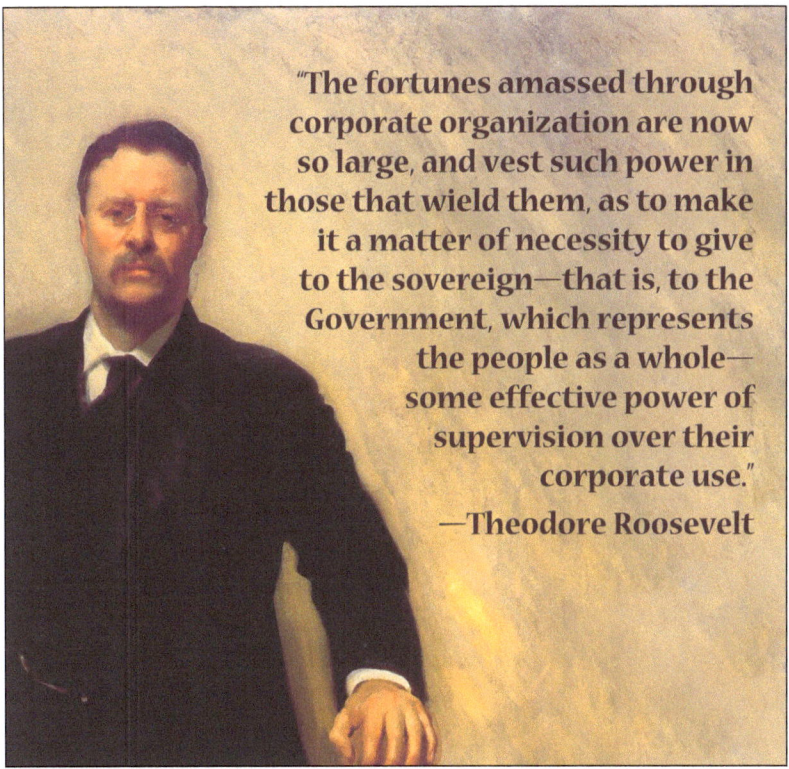

"The fortunes amassed through corporate organization are now so large, and vest such power in those that wield them, as to make it a matter of necessity to give to the sovereign—that is, to the Government, which represents the people as a whole—some effective power of supervision over their corporate use."
—Theodore Roosevelt

- To avoid chopping a sentence with more than one pair of dashes, it's often better to use parentheses to set off short appositional phrases:

  The smaller infractions (illegal campaign loans, influence-peddling) might be overshadowed by the major crimes (insider trading, bribery) in the media.

- Appositional phrases can be set off with commas, parentheses, or dashes. In general, commas are used when the flow is least interrupted by the apposition; dashes, when the apposition is most abrupt. "The parenthesis," in Trimble's words, "takes over when some incidental information—an explanation or amplification—wants to be slipped into the sentence in the form of a low-voiced aside, or when it is not grammatically part of the sentence and so must be walled off from it."

"It's time for greatness—not for greed. It's a time for idealism—not ideology. It is a time not just for compassionate words, but compassionate action."
—Marian Wright Edelman

The poison of skepticism becomes, like alcoholism, tuberculosis, and some other diseases, much more virulent in a hitherto virgin soil.
— Simone Weil

"This letter (a copy is enclosed) explains the school board's position."

- Dashes are substituted for commas when commas might mislead the reader:

Dash

> The cats—dogs and birds would be fed later—were taken into the kitchen.

In this example, commas might lead us to believe that the comma after *cats* signaled the beginning of a series.

- Similarly, if commas are used to mark minor divisions within the appositional phrase, dashes are used to set off the entire apposition to avoid confusion:

  > The first load of horses—appaloosas, bays, and roans—came off the van easily enough.

- When a parenthetical element set off by dashes requires a question mark or exclamation point itself, such punctuation may be retained before the second dash:

  > At this point, Waldo—what could he have been thinking about?—turned and stormed out.

To avoid confusion, no more than a single dash or a single pair of dashes should be used in a sentence. Also, to avoid a glut of punctuation, dashes shouldn't be used in the same sentence with colons. The careful writer normally refrains from using major punctuation (dash, colon, parentheses) more than once in a paragraph, thus avoiding stylistic confusion or overload.

Ellipses

Ellipsis points indicate an omission of a word or words in a quotation, a lapse of time, or a pause. Note that in the following examples, spaces are used between the periods to achieve maximum typographical harmony.

- An omission of a word or words in the middle of a sentence calls for an ellipsis of three spaced periods:

    Success is a rare paint . . . [it] hides all the ugliness.
    —John Suckling

    Men have money not because they are smarter . . . but because they have devoted such intellect as the Lord gave them to the base purpose of acquiring wealth.
    —Clarence Darrow

    The worst sin . . . is . . . to be indifferent.
    —George Bernard Shaw

    Money . . . ranks with love as man's greatest joy. And it ranks with death as his greatest source of anxiety.
    —John Kenneth Galbraith

    "Belief alone is nothing to be proud of . . . Belief without evidence is the very hallmark of the savage . . . No man is capable of greater evil than the one who thinks himself in the right. No purpose more evil than the higher purpose. . . ."
    —Joe Abercrombie

- An ellipsis at the end of a sentence needs a final punctuation mark (with a space preceding it). But if the sentence is broken where a comma punctuated the original, drop the comma. (Ellipsis points cover omitted punctuation as well as text.) Note that at the end of a sentence, no space precedes the initial period of the ellipsis:

> Fred Fosco once said, "She is so polite as to be frustrating. . . ."

> Great men, great nations, have not been boasters and buffoons, but perceivers of the terror of life. . . .
> —Ralph Waldo Emerson

Observe that no space precedes a closing quotation mark, either.

- Ellipses indicating an omission at the beginning of a quote are marked with three spaced periods, including a space before the initial word, which is capitalized. Often, though, you can avoid the clutter of ellipsis dots by merging a truncated quotation right into your sentence. The first word of the quotation, being lowercase, silently indicates an ellipsis:

> Part of the Presbyterian service asked forgiveness "for pretending to care for the poor, when we do not like poor people and do not want them in our homes."
> —United Presbyterian Church, Litany for Holy Communion

> James Bryce noted that for most of us, "nothing is more troublesome than the effort of thinking."
> —James Bryce

- Three periods, with no end punctuation, are used at the end of a quoted sentence that is deliberately and grammatically incomplete. As in other examples, a space precedes the first period, though no space is used between the last period and the quotation mark:

> We all know that the declaration reads, "When, in the course of human events . . ." But what follows that?

- Ellipses can be used to indicate a lapse of time or a pause too long to be indicated by a dash:

> "Yes, a busted water pump . . . tricky thing to replace . . . if we even have one."

Ellipses

"A religion true to its nature must also be concerned about man's social conditions. . . . Any religion that professes to be concerned with the souls of men and is not concerned with the slums that damn them, the economic conditions that strangle them, and the social conditions that cripple them is a dry-as-dust religion."

—Martin Luther King Jr.

- When ellipsis points are used at the end of a sentence in a quote that trails off, the writer must decide whether the sentence is to be construed as incomplete (three periods) or complete (three periods plus end punctuation):

    "I didn't think . . ."

    "I didn't know you cared. . . ."

Ellipses seem to suggest faltering or fragmented speech accompanied by confusion, insecurity, distress, or uncertainty. Dashes suggest abrupt changes in thought or impatient fractures of grammar without confusion or indecisiveness:

    "I . . . I . . . that is, we . . . blew it."

    "But . . . but . . ."

"The poverty of our century is unlike that of any other. It is not, as poverty was before, the result of natural scarcity, but of a set of priorities imposed upon the rest of the world by the rich. Consequently, the modern poor are not to be pitied . . . but written off as trash. The twentieth-century consumer economy has produced the first culture for which a beggar is a reminder of nothing."
—John Berger

- In telephone conversations where only one side is given, ellipses are generally used to indicate pauses for the other side of the conversation.

    "She did *what?*" . . . "When did this happen?"

Exclamation Points

Known as "screamers," exclamation points can be used effectively in certain situations, but should be used sparingly. This much-abused mark of punctuation is a favorite of the advertising fraternity. Admen emblazon every mundane statement with an exclamation, in hopes of implanting excitement: "New!" "Now! For the first time!" "Ultra dessert topping!" This, of course, bears no relationship to careful writing.

⚙ The exclamation point can be used after a command, an expression of strong feeling, or an otherwise forceful utterance:

> Critics! Those cut-throat bandits in the paths of fame.
> —Robert Burns

> Happy he who learns to bear what he cannot change!
> —Johann Schiller

> Poor fool! in whose petty estimation all things are little.
> —Johann Wolfgang von Goethe

> Alas! all music jars when the soul's out of tune.
> — Miguel de Cervantes

> Love in a hut, with water and a crust, / Is—Love, forgive us!—cinders, ashes, dust.
> —John Keats

⚙ Sometimes it may be used to indicate irony in a sentence, but here again it should be used sparingly:

> How I like to be liked, and what I do to be liked!
> —Charles Lamb

> How many learned men are working at the forge of science—laborious, ardent, tireless Cyclopes, but one-eyed!
> —Joseph Joubert

"It is money, money, money! Not ideas, not principles, but money that reigns supreme in American politics."
—Robert Byrd

O, what men dare do! what men may do! what men daily do, not knowing what they do!

—William Shakespeare

On occasion, the exclamation point may serve at the end of an indirect question to provide a little strength:

It couldn't be her!

Uh-oh. What now!

Exclamation Points

- The exclamation point should be placed inside the quotation marks, parentheses, or brackets when it's part of the quoted or parenthetical matter; otherwise, it should be placed outside.

    > The sudden change in personality reminded me of a passage from Robert Browning: "God be thanked, the meanest of his creatures / Boasts two soul-sides, one to face the world with, / One to show a woman when he loves her!"
    > —Robert Browning

- Sometimes a declarative sentence is to be read as an exclamation and is punctuated accordingly:

    > Maidens' hearts are always soft: Would that men's were truer!
    > —William Cullen Bryant

    > How sharper than a serpent's tooth it is / To have a thankless child!
    > —William Shakespeare

Hyphens

Stylebooks vary widely in their rules for hyphens, making it little more than a judgment call, oftentimes. This free-for-all mentality led the Oxford University Press to state, in their stylebook, "If you take hyphens seriously, you will surely go mad." Nonetheless, we offer the following guidelines:

- Modern newspaper (and some magazine) style dictates that you don't need to compound words (by hyphenating) if they appear in regular order, their meaning is clear (no alternate meaning is possible), and their comprehension wouldn't be improved by compounding:

    high school dance, city hall denizen, city council retreat

    A noble thought, but we feel that this rule is massively abused. Writers today pile five, six, or more adjectives in front of a noun, losing readers in a tangled morass of verbiage. *Where's the noun? How should this be read?* We believe the careful writer should use hyphens to guide readers through the swamp, making it clear which pairs (or groups) of words are to be read as a unit.

    The real world is not user-friendly
    — Kelvin Throop

- Many stylebooks, we feel, confuse the issue when dealing with a compound modifier made up of a noun, adjective, or adverb plus a present participle (*free-swinging, good-looking*), or an adjective plus past participle (*high-powered, fresh-picked*), or the past participle formed by adding *-d* or *-ed* to a noun (*able-bodied, full-blooded*). They state that if the compound precedes the noun

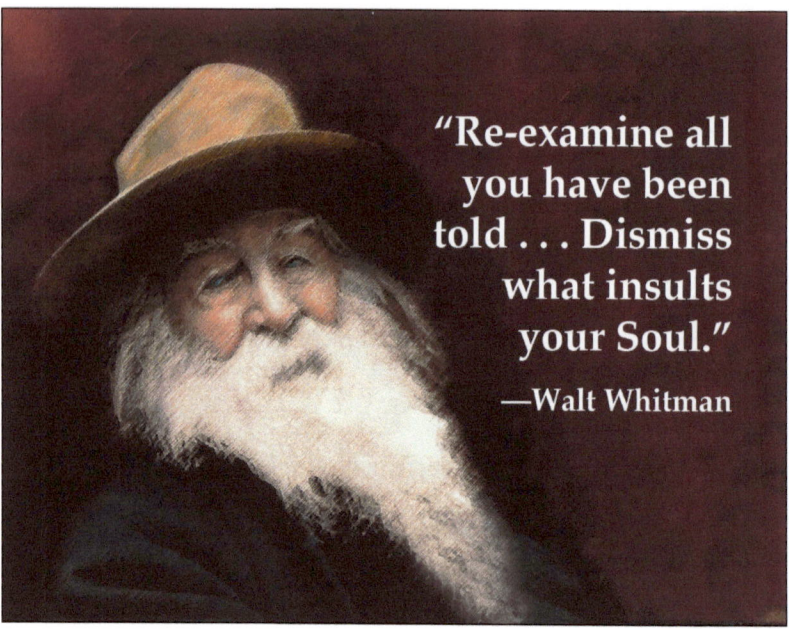

"Re-examine all you have been told ... Dismiss what insults your Soul."

—Walt Whitman

it modifies, it requires hyphenation, but not when it follows the noun in the sentence:

Before: The full-blooded Cherokee ...
After: The Cherokee is full blooded.

This distinction strikes us as inconsistent. We have no quarrel with the rationale for hyphenating a compound modifier *before* the noun. In "full-blooded Cherokee," you hyphenate because the parts of the modifier depend on each other for meaning. You wouldn't say "full Cherokee" or "blooded Cherokee." The modifier is understandable only as a unit, "full-blooded." As commonsensical as this is, why shouldn't the same rationale apply when the modifier appears at the back of a sentence? You wouldn't say "the Cherokee is full" or "the Cherokee is blooded." Clearly, the modifier again acts as a unit: "The Cherokee is full-blooded." And just as clearly, the hyphen is needed to signal the compound. This way of thinking might cost us invitations to some of the better tea parties, but so be it.

These same stylebooks further confound the issue by saying that some of these compounds take a hyphen after the noun—you

Hyphens

figure it out which these are (aside from a couple examples they provide). Once again, we favor the "one rule fits all" approach; any further muddling of the laws governing the English language is properly the work of Mrs. Thistlebottom's Hobgoblins.

- Similarly, many stylebooks say that compounds formed with words such as *well, ill, better, best,* and *lesser* sport hyphens only when they appear before the noun. And again, we feel the reader's interest is best served by a hyphen, no matter the geographical location of a compound. If, however, the compound itself is modified (as in "very well known man"), no hyphens are used.

- In general, compound words to avoid ambiguity in reading, to clarify figurative or improvised usage, and *to express a single thought that the words do not express when used separately:*

    pay-as-you-go plan, happy-go-lucky guy, small-business profits, forget-me-not

    Use a hyphen to join prepositional-phrase compounds of three or more words used to convey a single sense:

    jack-in-the-box, mother-of-pearl, stick-in-the-mud (but: flash in the pan)

- Compound verb forms are usually hyphenated:

    to soft-pedal, to cold-shoulder

- Similarly, compound noun forms are hyphenated:

    high-roller, do-gooder

    A compound noun form also must be hyphenated if a prefix or suffix is added:

    measuring-cupfuls, oil-tankerful

- In general, hyphenate a compound if it is used adjectivally before a noun, but dispense with hyphens if it's used adverbially:

    "... a 54-to-21 vote."

    "The Senate voted, 54 to 21, to ..."

- Don't hyphenate a compound modifier whose first word is an adverb ending in *-ly*, for such a word is clearly an adverb and modifies the word following it:

    eagerly awaited speech, totally inept performance

    But: Some words ending in *-ly* are *not* adverbs, such as the adjective "scholarly." Such words are treated conventionally (e.g., "He was a scholarly-looking man"). The test: If the word can be used as an adjective *by itself* (e.g., "the scholarly man"), it takes a hyphen in the compound form.

- Don't hyphenate foreign phrases used as modifiers unless they're hyphenated in the original:

    ante bellum days, per diem allowance, a priori decision (but: laissez-faire capitalism)

- In a compound modifier, the suspensive hyphen links the elements:

    one- and two-bedroom houses, 15- and 20-foot boats

    But most stylebooks (this one included) caution against using the suspensive hyphen as follows:

    The measure was killed in a well-timed and -executed maneuver.

- Use a hyphen with *ex-* when it means "former," and join it with the noun, not a modifier:

    ex-secretary, ex-director of HUD (not ex-HUD director)

- Use a hyphen to avoid doubling vowels except after short prefixes like *co-, de-, pre-, pro-,* and *re-*:

    anti-inflation, micro-organism, semi-independent (but: cooperate, deemphasize, preempt)

    Sometimes, however, the hyphen must be used to avoid confusion:

    co-own (a joint effort), re-cover (to cover again), re-collect (collect again), re-lease (lease again)

- Use a hyphen to join prefixes to capitalized words unless the combined form has acquired independent meaning:

Hyphens

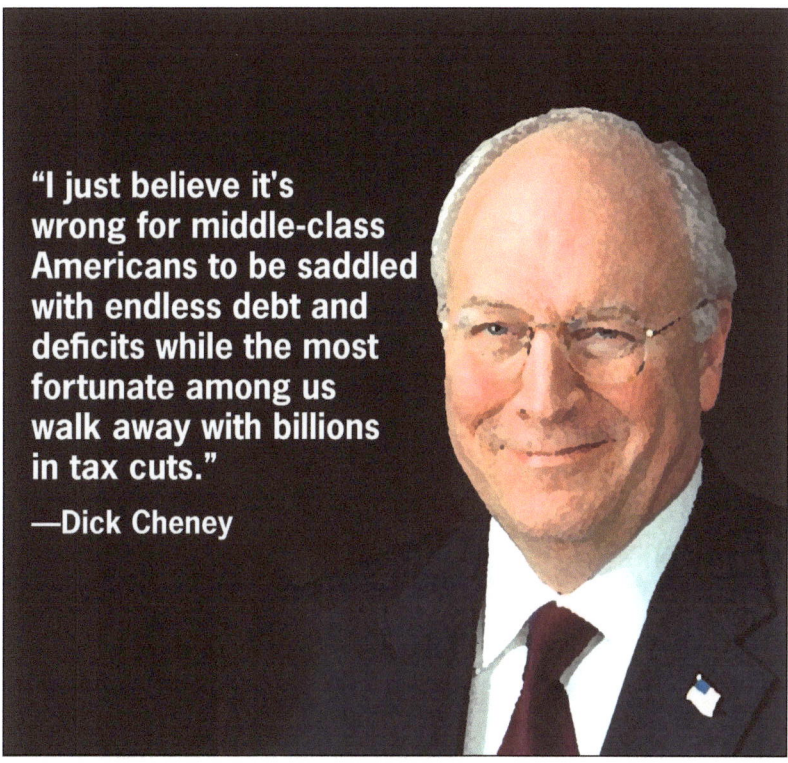

"I just believe it's wrong for middle-class Americans to be saddled with endless debt and deficits while the most fortunate among us walk away with billions in tax cuts."
—Dick Cheney

anti-British, un-American, pre-Columbian (but: transatlantic, antisemitic)

- Don't use a hyphen in titles except to indicate combined offices or non-incumbency:

    vice president, secretary of state, attorney general, ambassador at large, editor in chief

    But: secretary-treasurer (combined offices), secretary-designate, ex-governor, president-elect (non-incumbency)

    When using *-elect*, if the office is more than one word, the hyphen is dropped, as in "assessor collector elect."

- Use a hyphen to indicate joint relationships:

    city-county cooperation, blue-green feathers, Taft-Hartley Act, author-critic, soldier-statesman, Spanish-American War

"In this age, the mere example of non-conformity, the mere refusal to bend the knee to custom, is itself a service."

—John Stuart Mill

- Use a hyphen to separate doubled prefixes, as in "re-redirect."
- Use a hyphen to join conflicting or repetitive elements:

    comedy-ballet, pitter-patter, walkie-talkie

- Use a hyphen to join a single capital letter to a noun or participle:

    H-bomb, T-shirt, U-boat, V-necked, X-ray

- Use a hyphen with figurative compound expressions using an apostrophe in the first word:

    bull's-eye, cat's-paw, crow's-nest, camel's-hair

- Use a hyphen to join compound numbers and fractions:

    6-4 forward, 4-1 odds, 20-20 vision, four ten-thousandths

    (but: 10 percent interest, $100 billion deficit)

    Note in the above examples that for fractions, the numerator and

Hyphens

denominator are joined by a hyphen unless one or the other is already hyphenated. Modern usage also now dictates that a simple fraction used as a noun is not hyphenated:

> One half of the gold is yours, the other half is mine.

- Use a hyphen to join modifiers in a number-word form (but not in word-number or letter-number form except for federal road numbers):

   > ten-inch margin, three-mile limit, six-year-old girl, 40-yard dash, 100-watt bulb, 12-foot header (but: uranium 235, Formula 1 racer, Mark IV, Rt. 66, US-40, I-35)

- Don't use a hyphen when a noun is modified by a word of relationship:

   > fellow man, father figure, parent organization

- Noun forms with *quasi* are not hyphenated, but adjectival forms are:

   > quasi government, quasi union, quasi-public dealings, quasi-judicial proceedings

- Close up all *grand* relatives:

   > grandmother, grandniece, grandnephew, granddaddy

- Hyphenate all in-laws:

   > mother-in-law, sisters-in-law, brother-in-law

- Hyphenate all *great-* add-ons (relatives):

   > great-grandfather, great-great-grandmother, great-aunt

- Hyphenate all words preceded by *self-*:

   > self-control, self-knowledge, self-conscious (but: unselfconscious)

- Hyphenate adjectival forms using *half-*:

   > half-baked plan, half-asleep, half-cocked

   > He appeared half-asleep.

- Spell compounds with *-ache* solid:

    headache, toothache

- Permanent compounds with *-book* are spelled solid (except for a few unwieldy ones):

    checkbook, textbook, notebook (but: phrase book, reference book)

    Permanent compounds with *-house* are spelled solid; temporary ones, open:

    clubhouse, townhouse, greenhouse (but: rest house)

    Compounds with *-boat, -fish, -keeper, -man, -mate, -owner, -proof, -room, -shop, -tight, -wise, -work,* and *-yard* are often spelled solid:

    houseboat, codfish, beekeeper, doorman, helpmate, homeowner, foolproof, bedroom, workshop, watertight, streetwise, homework, backyard

- In adjective form, adverbs other than *-ly* types plus participle or adjective use the hyphen:

    long-lived career, much-loved man, ever-fruitful tree, still-active oldster

- Chemical terms do not require hyphens:

    hydrogen peroxide solution, sulfuric acid mix, uranium 235 core

- Generally, compound color terms, as modifiers, take hyphens:

    blue-green algae, red-green color blindness, black-and-white print

    The last example illustrates a convention we favor. In the phrase "red and green vases," no hyphens are used if there are red vases and green vases. Hyphens are added if the vases are two-color.

- When *-odd* is tacked on to a cardinal number, a hyphen is required:

    20-odd shows, 45-odd people

- Compounds with *high-* and *low-* normally take hyphens:

    high-level talks, low-rent building (but: highbrow, lowbred)

Hyphens

- Phrases used as adjectives are hyphenated, unless they are already enclosed in quotation marks:

  "one rule fits all" approach, a can-do city council, "Gone With the Wind" typecasting, an every-man-for-himself attitude

  Note: As a rule, proper nouns or adjectives are not hyphenated:

  Mickey Mouse rules, Old World ambiance

- Any temporary adjectival forms using *cross-* are hyphenated:

  cross-country race, cross-cut saw

- Compounds with *all-* take hyphens:

  all-inclusive study, all-around jock, all-powerful, all-American

- The suffix *-like* is freely used to form new compounds, and is generally spelled solid except for those words formed from proper names, words ending in *-ll*, and word combinations. Some copyeditors also prefer to hyphenate when the base word ends in a single *-l* or consists of three or more syllables.

  catlike reflexes, meatlike, saillike or sail-like (always: Bronx-like, bell-like, can-opener-like)

- Adjectival compounds with *-fold* are spelled solid unless they are formed with figures:

  twofold, tenfold (but: 15-fold increase)

- A word denoting a geographical, political, or social division plus *-wide* is spelled closed unless the compound is long and cumbersome:

  statewide vote, worldwide acclaim, citywide tussle (but: archdiocese-wide)

- Suffixes tend to run together with the root word, but sometimes a hyphen must be used to clarify:

  makeup, pickup truck, lean-to, mop-up operation

Parentheses

 Many times, dashes or parentheses are equally good style, but parentheses are normally reserved for enclosing text having no essential connection to the rest of the sentence.

> Silence will save me from being wrong (and foolish), but it will also deprive me of the possibility of being right.
> —Igor Stravinsky

> Men are apt to offend ('tis true) where they find most goodness to forgive.
> —William Congreve

If matter enclosed in parentheses is a complete declarative or imperative sentence—cast within a complete sentence—the period is omitted. But any other punctuation mark called for by the construction may be used.

> The whole essence of true gentle breeding (one does not like to say gentility) lies in the wish and the art to be agreeable.
> —Oliver Wendell Holmes Sr.

Parentheses may be used for a number of useful purposes:

a. incidental comment:

> If riches are, as Bacon says, the baggage ("impedimenta") of virtue ... poverty is famine in its commissary department, starving it into weakness for the great conflict of life.
> —Tryon Edwards

b. nicknames:

> Julius ("Doctor J") Erving

c. fuller identification:

> "I told [Judge Roy] Donovan that he was wrong."

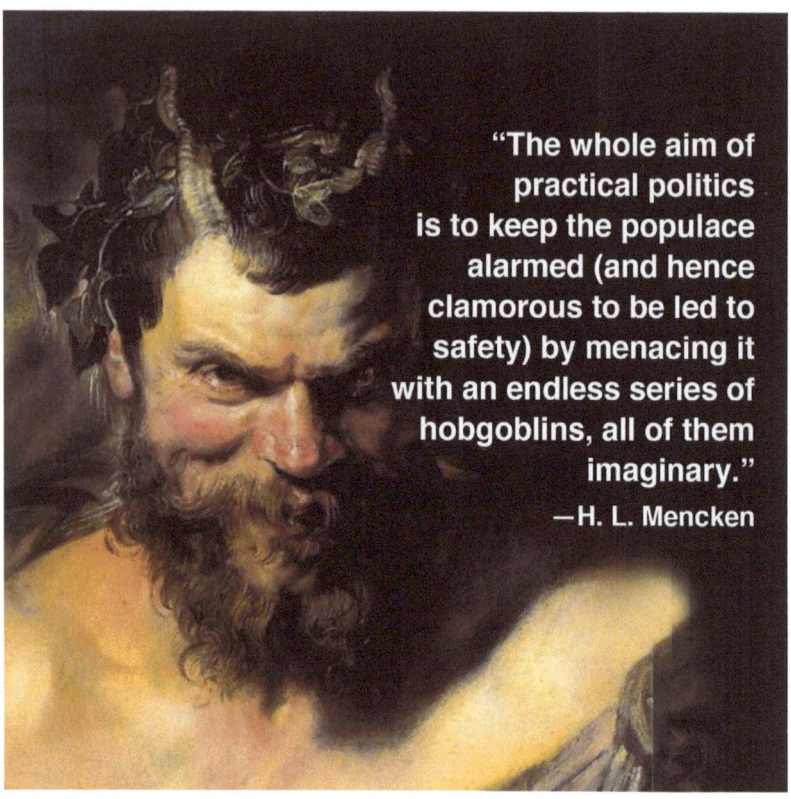

"The whole aim of practical politics is to keep the populace alarmed (and hence clamorous to be led to safety) by menacing it with an endless series of hobgoblins, all of them imaginary."
—H. L. Mencken

Note that when material is inserted into quotations, brackets are used, not parentheses, in most up-style publications. Others use parentheses.

d. political-geographical designation:

In Waco (north of Austin), the Baptists hold sway.

e. specific locations in ambiguous designations:

He arrived in Rochester (New York).

f. equivalents and translations:

It cost 1,700 pesos ($1) back then.

The Diet (parliament) went into conference.

g. explanatory material:

> "Many a profound genius ... is yet every day posed [baffled] by trivial questions at his own supper table," wrote Emerson.
> —Ralph Waldo Emerson

- In quoted matter, modern style calls for the use of dashes, not parentheses, to set off incidental comments and asides:

> "What they call happiness—and what Freud calls satisfaction of needs that have been dammed up—leaves me feeling empty," he said.
> —Sigmund Freud

- Occasionally, a combination of parentheses and dashes may be used to distinguish two overlapping parenthetical elements, each of which interrupts the continuity :

> He said then—and he appeared to be (at least somewhat) coherent—that he would play in the second half.

Periods

- Don't use a period after a complete sentence enclosed in either parentheses or quotation marks when that sentence is interpolated in another one:

    The middle-class qualities (I refrain from saying virtues) that the aspiring, climbing members of the working class display are rewarded in the world.

- When a period used as an abbreviation mark ends a sentence that is a question, use both marks:

    Do you ever use the notation *et al.?*

- Omit periods in most uppercase abbreviations:

    CIA, FBI, AFL-CIO, NFL (but: U.S., D.A., D.C., U.N.)

Question Marks

- *How* or *why*, within a sentence, need not be followed by a question mark. Often, these words are italicized:

    He asked himself why.

    It became a question of *how* rather than *when*.

- In rare instances, a question mark or exclamation point is part of the title of a work, such as a play or book, and it must be retained. This can be avoided by rewriting:

    "Didn't she star in the Broadway production of *Hello, Dolly!?*" he asked. (Better: "Didn't she star in *Hello, Dolly!* on Broadway?")

- If a question and an exclamation end together in a sentence, retain the stronger mark. This is not always apparent from the sentence, so choose the feeling that you wish to convey with the sentence:

    How would you react if I walked up to you and screamed, "You're fired!"

Semicolons

- Don't try to join anything less than complete sentences with a semicolon. As Trimble notes in *Writing With Style,* "If you can replace your semicolon with a period, your construction is okay."

    Said Faulkner, "If a writer has to rob his mother, he will not hesitate; the 'Ode to a Grecian Urn' is worth any number of old ladies."
    —Jean Stein

    Our faith comes in moments; our vice is habitual.
    —Ralph Waldo Emerson

    It is not enough to do good; one must do it the right way.
    —John Morley

    Wit has truth in it; wisecracking is simply calisthenics with words.
    — Dorothy Parker

    The whole life is but a point of time; let us enjoy it, therefore, while it lasts, and not spend it to no purpose.
    —Plutarch

    You must not lose faith in humanity. Humanity is an ocean; if a few drops of the ocean are dirty, the ocean does not become dirty.
    — Mahatma Gandhi

    Knowledge is proud that it knows so much; Wisdom is humble that it knows no more.
    — William Cowper

    We never live, but we hope to live; and as we are always arranging to be happy, it must be that we never are so.
    — Blaise Pascal

Man is certainly stark mad; he cannot make a flea, and yet he will be making gods by dozens.
—Michel de Montaigne

Propaganda does not deceive people; it merely helps them to deceive themselves.
—Eric Hoffer

Beware of false knowledge; it is more dangerous than ignorance.
—George Bernard Shaw

The golden moments in the stream of life rush past us, and we see nothing but sand; the angels come to visit us, and we only know them when they are gone.
—George Eliot

He who loses wealth loses much; he who loses a friend loses more; but he that loses his courage loses all.
— Miguel de Cervantes

Do not be too moral. You may cheat yourself out of much life. So aim above morality. Be not simply good; be good for something.
— Henry David Thoreau

The elliptical construction appears to violate the above rule, but a comma often substitutes for missing words:

In action, be primitive; in foresight, a strategist.
—Rene Char

Peace is the happy, natural state of man; war, his corruption, his disgrace.
—James Thomson

Men marry to make an end; women to make a beginning.
— Alexis Dupuy

The wealth of a soul is measured by how much it can feel; its poverty by how little.
— William R. Alger

- The following are considered adverbs rather than conjunctions and should be preceded by a semicolon when used transitionally—*then, however, thus, hence, indeed, accordingly, besides, therefore, nevertheless:*

Semicolons

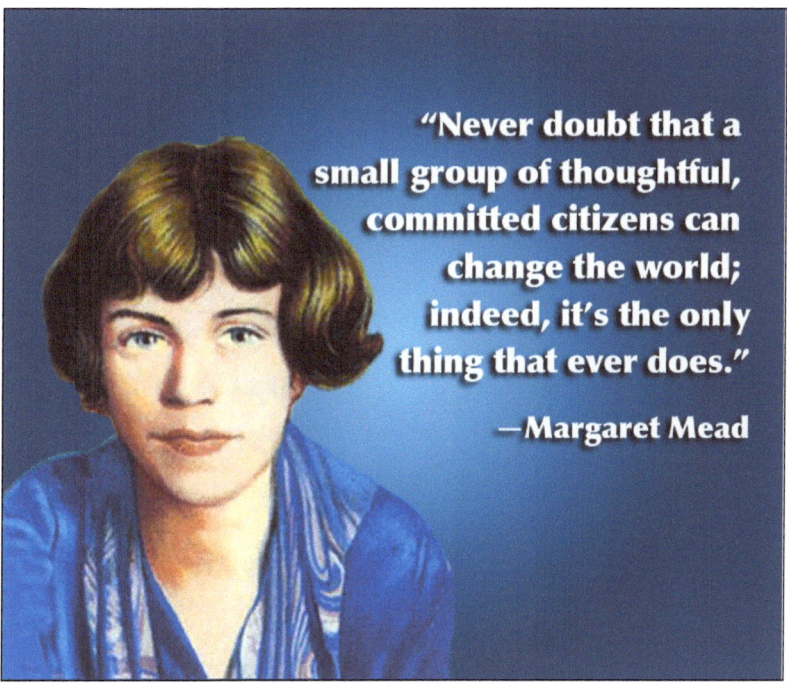

"Never doubt that a small group of thoughtful, committed citizens can change the world; indeed, it's the only thing that ever does."

—Margaret Mead

The flower you single out is a rejection of all other flowers; nevertheless, only on these terms is it beautiful.
—Saint-Exupery

- Semicolons are always placed outside of quotation marks or parentheses:

    He assumed everybody watched "Dancing With the Stars"; he never missed it.

- As one lone exception to the first and prevailing rule, the semicolon may be used to separate the elements in a list, particularly when commas might lead to confusion:

    Every great scientific truth goes through three states: First, people say it conflicts with the Bible; next, they sat it has been discovered before; lastly, they say they always believed it.
    —Louis Agassiz

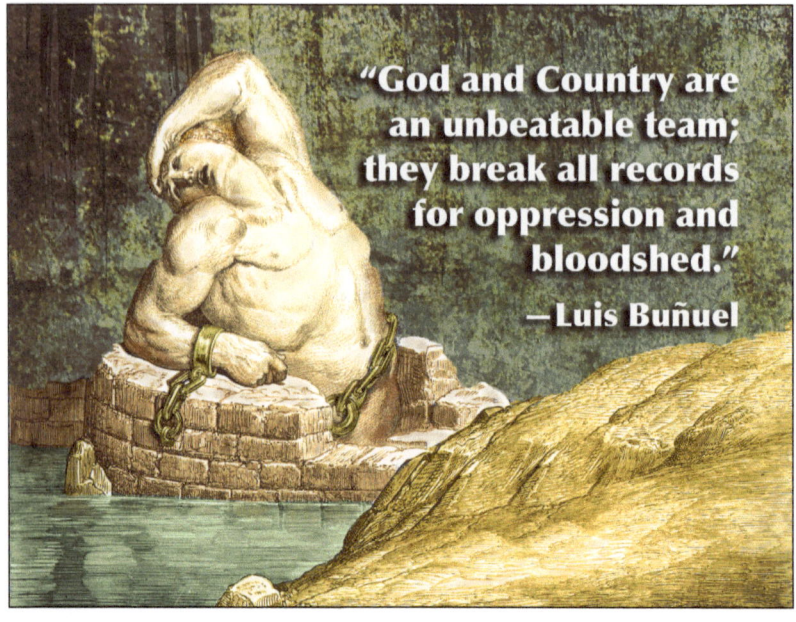

"God and Country are an unbeatable team; they break all records for oppression and bloodshed."
—Luis Buñuel

Some of the more fatuous flag-waving Americans are in danger of forgetting that you can't extract gratitude as you would extract a tooth; that unless friendship is freely given, it means nothing and less than nothing.

—Max Lerner

Compromise makes a good umbrella, but a poor roof; it is temporary expedient, often wise in party politics, almost sure to be unwise in statesmanship.

—James Russell Lowell

Acknowledgments

I am beholden to Dr. John R. Trimble, author of *Writing With Style: Conversations on the Art of Writing* (3e), for his forbearance in dealing with a zealot intent on defining some immutable rules of punctuation ("Age considers; youth ventures," Tagore). Language, of course, is fluid and defies regimentation, though that never deterred me from seeking some sense of order in the clutter. And thus I prevailed upon the doyen of careful writing for his expert advice.

The bulk of the text herein stems from sessions in his office during the 1980s. I bear sole responsibility for any revision and rewriting—including added art and quotes, as well as typos, inconsistencies, or ill-considered examples.

Craig Hattersley is a writer, editor, sometime handyman, and overall ne'er-do-well with a penchant for political discourse. He graduated summa cum laude from UT with a BS in journalism, and was senior editor at *3rd Coast* magazine, *Texas Life* magazine, and *Austin Weekly*, as well as writing or working for the *Village Voice*, Texas Monthly Publications, and the *Texas Observer*, among others. Additionally, he worked at G&S Typesetters in Austin, specializing in the production of college textbooks, before becoming communications director for the Texas Criminal Defense Lawyers Association. A misspent youth featured seven years under the hood working as a mechanic in a Volkswagen dealership, which might explain his passion for using the right tool for the job.

www.ingramcontent.com/pod-product-compliance
Lightning Source LLC
LaVergne TN
LVHW010019070426
835507LV00001B/4